Hi,
Thelma here!

I used to be a farm pony in a band with my friends . . .

. . . until some paint, glitter, and a carrot turned me into a UNICORN!

After that,
my band got our
BIG BREAK!

We got to meet really cool people . . .

. . . like
PEGGY
PURVIS . . .

. . . and VIC DIAMOND, too.

Okay, he wasn't that cool.

It was a
WILD RIDE!

THELMA THE UNICORN

Movie Novelization

THELMA THE UNICORN

Movie Novelization

By Kate Howard

Scholastic Inc.

ISBN 978-93-5954-338-3

First printing 2024

This reprint edition : June 2024

Printed in India at MicroPrints India, New Delhi

Book design by Martha Maynard

Chapter 1

The roar of the crowd was deafening. While the band tuned their instruments and prepared to wow their fans, the auditorium thrummed with excitement. This was it—the singer all these people had been waiting their whole lives to see . . .

THELMA!

The time had finally come for Thelma and her best-friends-slash-bandmates, Otis and Reggie, to perform live on the biggest stage, the best stage, *the* stage—the one and only Sparkle-Palooza! The crowd was cheering wildly, waiting for the concert's headline act: the one and only Thelma and her legendary band, the Rusty Buckets.

Thelma nestled into her favorite spot, standing confidently right at center stage, and pushed her snout up to the mic. "Sparkle-Palooza!" she crooned. "Give it up for the world's next big musical legends . . . *One, two, three, four!*"

With a final smile for the crowd, Thelma leaned into the mic and began to sing. She let herself relax into her music. She could feel the crowd cheering, pushing her on, into the heart of her song.

The Rusty Buckets were totally *on.* They had never sounded so good. This was the moment they'd been waiting for—their chance to finally headline Sparkle-Palooza—and they were owning it.

"And now," Thelma said as she strutted across her stage, "over here on lead guitar, my best friend, the Six String Slayer himself—Otis!"

Otis leaned into his guitar and began his solo. "Woo-hoo!" he cheered. "I'm gonna melt your face off! Ahh!"

With a grin, Thelma turned to her other best friend and bandmate. "And over here on drums," she crooned, "the Master of the Beat—Reggie!"

Reggie looked up from his drums and bleated, "I'm a donkey." He pounded away on his drums, saying nothing more.

"Okaaay," Thelma said, laughing. "I thought he'd say a little more than that."

Settling back into her spot at center stage, Thelma took up the mic again and prepared to wow her adoring fans. She tilted her nose up and said, "Now, finally, I write the songs, I sing the songs, and my name is—Thelma!" She grinned widely and added, "And *we* are the Rusty Buckets!"

The crowd whooped and hollered. Fire blasted out of the edge of the stage as the Rusty Buckets prepared to light the place up with their performance.

Reggie turned to Otis. "Hey, Otis," he said. "Do you know what time it is?"

"Ooh!" Otis whooped. "I know what time it is. Thelma, do *you* know what time it is?"

"Heck yeah, I know what time it is!" Thelma yelled.

She backed up to give herself space to get a running start. Thelma braced herself for liftoff as the crowd began to chant, "Thelma! Thelma! Thelma!"

Thelma raced across the stage as her bandmates and the crowd cheered her on. At the edge of the stage, Thelma leapt up into the air and, with all four legs splayed out like a starfish flew out to land in the crowd's waiting arms. She could hear cries of "We love you, Thelma!" coming from the sea of voices below her. Her face was a picture of joy, and her mane rippled behind her as she practically floated in midair over the crowd.

But then Thelma looked down—just in time to see the crowd split in two beneath her. Just moments before, thousands of adoring fans had been waiting to catch her, but now there was nothing except—

"Huh?" Thelma gasped, then landed with a loud thud on a scratchy bale of hay.

Chapter 2

"Ouch," Thelma said, wiggling her backside as she checked to see if anything on her body was broken. "We need softer hay."

Otis and Reggie both jumped off their band's makeshift barn stage and ran to their friend's side. Make-believe was always fun . . . until someone got hurt. As soon as it was clear that Thelma was just shaken up and not badly hurt, Reggie bleated, "That was *sick*!"

"Yeah!" Otis agreed. "You got, like, three feet of air that time!"

Thelma groaned as she pushed herself up to standing. "Well, I hope the judges like it. I just busted my tailbone, dude."

“Can I be real with you?” Reggie asked his bandmates. “If we really wanna kill this audition tomorrow, we’re gonna need some pyrotechnics. I got a big guy right here!”

Then Thelma spotted the *TNT* label on what Reggie had in his hoof—dynamite! And it was *lit*! “Wait, wait, wait?! Oh!”

Unbothered, Reggie tossed his lit stick of dynamite out of the barn with a quick flick of his hoof. It landed inside a porta-potty out on the barn lawn. The dynamite went off and the porta-potty flew up into the air, blasting sky-high like a rocket.

“Whoa,” Reggie said, his eyes wide as he watched the toilet soar through the air.

“Welp,” Thelma said, cringing as the porta-potty made its way back toward the ground. This wasn’t going to end well. “See you guys at work tomorrow! Bye!”

“Go, go, go,” Otis urged, shooing both his friends away from the scene of the crime.

They all scrambled to race out of the barn and across the farm’s fields. Thelma spun around just in time to see the toilet land hard. The door popped open, and a man rolled out onto the ground. He dusted himself off, muttering, “What in the heck was that?!”

Chapter 3

The next day, Thelma arrived for her usual shift at Pam's Dairy Farm. She clocked in, same as always.

"Mornin', Thelma," a farmer greeted her as she made her way toward her station.

"Mornin', Bob," Thelma said cheerfully. She passed some cows, then walked into the heart of the workplace action. "Hey, Bessie," she said, calling out to one of the cows. "I thought you had the week off?!"

Bessie shook her head. "Nope. People gotta have their cheese!"

Thelma laughed. "Girl, you crack me up, getting all that overtime. I hear you, I see you."

When she got out to the barnyard, Otis raced up

to his best pal and cheered. "Thelmaaa! Woop-*woop*!"

"Hey, Otis," Thelma said, grinning back at him. "Whatchu doin', how you feelin'?"

Otis held up his hoof so he and Thelma could do their signature hoof-shake. Thelma laughed as they wrapped it up with their classic booty-bump. Thelma loved being friends with Otis—they just *got* each other, and that's what best friends were all about. "So," Otis said as they buckled down for their day's work. "You ready for the big audition tonight?"

"Yeah, I'm ready!" Thelma whooped. "Let's do the dang thang! We've been trying to hit it big for way too long."

"Oh, come on," Otis said, tilting his head to one side. "It hasn't been *that* long."

Thelma gave him a look. "It's been ten years!" she argued. That was practically a lifetime! Thelma had been waiting for her big break forever, and she was about to get her chance to make it big—with the Rusty Buckets by her side, no less! "Don't you finally want to play somewhere that matters?"

Otis shrugged. "I'm happy playing music anywhere. As long as it's with you."

Thelma couldn't help but smile. Otis really was the

best kind of friend. She booty-bumped him again as they set off across the farm to their stations.

Suddenly, Reggie called out from somewhere across the farm. "Thelma, watch out!"

Thelma looked up just in time to see Reggie blasting toward her on the back of a tractor. His mane was covering his eyes, and the tractor was on a collision course with the barn. "Whoa!" Thelma said, ducking for cover. "You tryin' to kill me, Reggie? You need to cut them bangs, son."

"My bad!" Reggie said with a wave and a glance back over his shoulder. Moments later, the tractor hit the edge of a chicken coop, sending the residents inside scurrying out to safety. "Ah, dang it," Reggie said, hanging his head low. "Not again."

Otis and Thelma cracked up as they headed toward the barn.

Inside the barn's tack room, Thelma stuffed her songbook into her locker for safekeeping during the workday. It had all her most important stuff inside—songs she'd been working on for years, including the one song she knew was gonna be great eventually, but that she hadn't quite finished yet. Before she could slam the locker door closed, the book fell open to a lyrics page filled with crossed out words and scribbled-over musical notes, and Otis gestured to it. "Hey," he said. "So how are those new lyrics comin' along?"

"What lyrics?" Thelma asked.

"You know," Otis said. "The lyrics for the one song you don't have lyrics for."

Thelma blinked. Then, with a laugh she said, "Come on, Otis, you know that has stumped me since I was a kid." Before they could talk about it further, Thelma held up a hoof and signaled for Otis to pipe down. Her favorite artist was on the TV, and she needed to know what it was all about! "Hold up, I gotta see this."

"And now," the TV host said. "The world premiere of the music video for Nikki Narwhal's latest song, 'Blubber Trouble'!"

Thelma and Otis stood side by side, catching the latest hit from the greatest superstar in the world—Nikki Narwhal! Thelma loved watching Nikki perform—in this video, a collection of dancing Pool Boys swarmed around Nikki as she sang and swatted them into the water. Thelma danced along, wishing she could experience a life of fame like Nikki Narwhal.

On-screen, Nikki had just pulled a chain hanging over her head, and now slimy seafood was raining down on her like jewels.

"Wow," Thelma said, swooning as she watched. "Now there's someone who has it all."

"No way," Otis grumbled. "Nikki's such a sellout. She's as fake as it gets!"

"Who cares?" Thelma argued. "That girl gets to sing at Sparkle-Palooza every year! That'll be us someday . . . I just know it."

"Hey, Thelma!" a groom yelled from somewhere outside the tack room, dragging the two friends' attention away from the TV. "Otis!"

With a sigh, Thelma called back, "Yeah, what do you want?" She and Otis popped their heads out of the tack room.

The groom gave them a meaningful look and said, "This manure isn't gonna move itself."

Nearby, a goat coworker looked helplessly at Thelma and said, "Yeah, Thelma. I can't work like this."

"Yeah, yeah," Thelma muttered. "I got you. I'm coming."

The rest of the day passed much like all the others that had come before. But even as she went through the same old, same old, at least Thelma had something big to look forward to—their audition! It was enough to keep her going through her whole shift of hauling manure.

Even when the flies tried their best to send her spiraling.

"Come on, Thelma," one fly whined. "Give us that manure!"

"Yeah, we're starving!" droned another.

Thelma shot the swarm a firm look and said, "Y'all better not be laying eggs in my hair!" She took a breath, sputtering when she realized she'd inhaled a fly.

"Ahhh!" the fly screamed.

Throwing herself to the ground, Thelma rolled around, huffing and snorting desperately to get the fly out of there.

"She's a fly eater!" one of the flies said, dive-bombing her.

"Get him out!" cried another.

"Fly eater!" the rest of them buzzed.

Finally, Thelma snorted hard and the fly shot out. As it lay dizzy and spinning on the ground, the snot-soaked fly sobbed, "I was in her brain! I was in her *brain*!"

Chapter 4

The day had gone from boring to worse, and Thelma wasn't feeling as hopeful and positive as she had been that morning. As she hauled manure through the pasture, she glanced over a nearby fence and spotted three glamorous horses and their human trainers headed her way. Seeing their fancy group made her feel even worse about herself.

Thelma ducked her head and whispered, "Oh no! Please don't see me, please don't see me, please don't see me." Scuttling backward, Thelma spun and ran—and then tripped on a rock. "Ah!" she grunted, her legs splayed in all directions on the ground. "Oof."

All the manure she'd been hauling spilled out and

covered her in a thick, stinky mess. Thelma was so covered in poop that she had to dig her way out, gasping for air when she finally made it to the surface.

"Look at that avalanche of doo-doo," Zirconia, one of the fancy horses, trilled out, laughing at Thelma's misfortune. "Done fell right on her!"

Zirconia's horse friends, Ruby and Sapphire, laughed hysterically, along with their human trainers, Esteban and Claudia. The five of them came over to the fence at the edge of their property for a closer view of Thelma's misfortune.

Thelma was tempted to hide under the pile of poop to save her from the humiliation of their comments and laughter.

"Thelma," Zirconia said haughtily. "Is this your routine for the audition tonight?"

"No, Zirconia," Thelma said, rolling her eyes. "You know I'm singing."

Zirconia laughed harder. "You gotta be joking. Ain't nobody on earth wanna hear music from a plain ole farm pony."

"You look disgusting!" Esteban added dramatically.

"Girl, we have the looks . . ." Zirconia said as she

and her friends all struck a pose. "*And* the talent." The three elegant horses shared high fives, preening and strutting past manure-covered, plain old Thelma.

"And you got nothing," Esteban added.

Thelma was sick of others treating her like this! It didn't matter what she looked like. All that mattered was *talent*, and she had plenty of that. She'd show them! With a mighty wriggle, Thelma shook the manure off herself and watched with glee as it splattered onto the group.

"Hey!" Esteban shrieked.

Thelma grinned, then looked meaningfully at Zirconia. "At least I don't have some crusty ole pink eye."

Then she turned and strutted away as Zirconia turned toward Esteban in a panic. "What?! Esteban, is she for real?!" She held her eye open with her hoof. "Do I have pink eye?"

Esteban winced as Zirconia brought her eye up close to his. "Yeah," he said reluctantly. "I think you do."

The entire farm could hear Zirconia's scream.

Chapter 5

Later that night, Thelma finally felt ready. The time had come for her to audition in front of everyone and show the world what she could do. As she stood backstage in a small arena filled with spectators, Thelma heard the emcee announce, "Opening tonight for our Sparkle-Palooza talent search, we bring you—the Rhinestone Fillies!"

Thelma winced as the three horses and their human trainers who'd been so cruel to her earlier in the day pranced out onto the stage. A spotlight was trained on one of the humans, Esteban, as upbeat music began to play. He shimmied to the beat as his partner, Claudia, lifted him onto Zirconia.

The crowd went wild as the three horses and their human handlers performed acrobatic stunts onstage. Unable to hold back his enthusiasm, Reggie began to cheer. Meanwhile, Otis and Thelma watched on, glum.

The horses formed a pyramid, prancing around in a circle while the humans danced around them. Thelma heard one of the judges quack encouragingly. Even her pal Reggie seemed to be totally into the performance, though this was probably the Rusty Buckets' biggest competition.

As the band approached the end of their number, Thelma's eyes narrowed when the horses launched the humans into the air and then somehow caught them without a single fumble. The crowd went wild, but even worse, the judges were eating it up. They all stood and clapped, and Thelma noticed they were all wiping tears from their eyes!

"Woo ya, that's what I'm talking about!" said one of the judges, as he and the other two judges all lifted signs with a giant number 10 written on them. Perfect scores! They'd gotten perfect scores! This meant the Rusty Buckets had to be perfect to stand a chance of winning.

Thelma turned to Otis, suddenly worried. "Otis,"

she whispered. "I'm so nervous, I feel like my heart's gonna drop outta my butt."

"That's scientifically impossible," Otis informed her.

"No, really," Thelma said, panicking. "I can feel it!"

Onstage, the llama emcee stepped up to the mic to address the crowd. "Oooee, next up on our talent search tonight, an original song performed by, uh . . ." He pulled out a program to check the order of the show. Thelma didn't think it was a good sign that he'd forgotten their band's name. Oh well . . . after they performed, no one would be able to forget their name again! The emcee stepped back from the mic and yelled, "The Rusty Buckets!"

Otis and Reggie unfurled their band's banner, releasing a cloud of flies and dust. Meanwhile, backstage, Thelma took one more look in the mirror. She flashed herself a smile, then strode out onto the stage, trying to look and feel confident. But as soon as she reached the microphone, she realized the mic stand was set way too high and now she looked tiny—and felt even tinier.

Before she could freak out, Otis kicked a wooden apple crate her way, winked, and whispered, "You got this."

With a grateful smile back at him, Thelma scrambled up onto the crate and settled in right in front of the mic. "Woo!" she said, greeting the crowd. "Ha ha, hey everybody!" The mic screeched with feedback, and Thelma took a breath. "Uh, we're the Rusty Buckets, and we're really excited—"

Before she could finish her sentence, one of the judges bleated out, "NEXT!"

"Wait," Thelma said. "Wait, what?"

"Off the stage, please," another judge said.

"But we didn't even get a chance to perform our song!" Thelma protested.

"I'm sorry, kid," the judge said, not sounding very sorry at all. "There's no future here, okay? Keep it movin'."

Thelma shook her head. "Hold up. We've waited years for this opportunity. What's not working for you?"

The judges looked at one another, exchanging awkward glances. "Ugh," one of them said. "Look, babe, you just don't have *it*."

"*It?*" Thelma asked, confused. "Whaddya mean?"

"We just want people with a certain *look*," the judge explained. "Someone that sparkles and lights up a stage. Not some forgettable farm pony."

Thelma's face fell. Was this what it was all about? What she *looked* like, not her talent? "What?" she asked, unwilling to accept that as the truth.

"Yo yo," one of the other judges said casually. "You've gotta be something special to perform at Sparkle-Palooza. I'm sorry, but you'll never perform there."

Thelma had had enough. This was ridiculous! Who were they to decide that her looks mattered more than her voice? "Now you listen here, buddy—" she began, but just as she started to really speak her mind, she lost her balance and awkwardly flopped off the wooden crate she'd been standing on. Her leg tangled into the long microphone cord, dragging all the band equipment right off the stage with her. The equipment landed on top of Thelma, and after a beat, the microphone and its stand followed, crashing down right on her head.

With the roar of a laughing crowd echoing in her ears, a thoroughly humiliated Thelma rushed off.

Chapter 6

Later that evening, Thelma sat glumly in a booth at her favorite roadside café, moping about the audition. She watched her performance, which had gone viral, replay over and over on her phone. Every time she watched it, the same words popped up over her face at the end of the video: *NEVER. GONNA. HAPPEN.*

Thelma's head drooped. Would it really *never* happen for them?

Suddenly a figurine—designed to look like a donkey barbarian—appeared right in front of her face. "Good evening, fair maiden," someone said in a silly voice that was meant to sound like whatever a donkey barbarian sounded like. "Why the long face? I have come from afar to cheer thee up. Wilt thou join me on a quest?"

Thelma sighed. It was just like her pal Otis to try to cheer her up with his silly characters and games. She'd play along, just like always. "Sure . . ."

Otis settled in across from his best pal, holding a box filled with even more figurines. "Let me transport you to a realm of goblins, sorcery, and nineteenth-century homesteaders on the Oregon Trail." Otis dumped the contents of his box onto the table, spilling warriors, goblins, pioneers, and covered wagons all over the space between him and Thelma. "It's a completely original role-playing game I've been developing. I call it . . . Dungeons and Wagons."

Noticing that Thelma wasn't yet smiling, Otis slid in next to her and showed her his donkey barbarian figurine up close. "My character is a donkey warlord named Donk-Truvius," he explained. He pointed at the figure's chest and said, "Check it out—he's got a fake nipple . . . that doubles as a ninja star!"

"Donk *who*?" Thelma asked, nearly smiling when the nipple on Donk-Truvius fell off and plopped onto the table with a quiet *plink*.

"Here," Otis said, handing Thelma a sad-looking

pony figurine. "This is your character. She's a hardened pioneer pony who dabbles in martial arts. She also just beat cholera, so she has super high stamina points. What do you want to call her?"

Thelma let out a long sigh. "*Pffft* . . . Horse Lady."

"Come on," Otis urged. "You can do better than that."

"Okay, fine," Thelma said. "Then *Sad* Horse Lady."

Otis groaned. "What? That's weak."

Thelma snagged a unicorn figurine off the table. "Why can't I just be this unicorn?"

"Oh, sorry," Otis said. "*Everyone* wants to be her. She's a level three hundred cleric. You can only unlock her after you sell your soul to a shape-shifter warlock." He rearranged the figurines, putting the pioneers around the wagons to ward off a made-up goblin attack. "Okay, okay," he said, getting excited to carry on in his story. "So, our wagon train has just been attacked by a horde of goblins and *we* are the only survivors!"

Thelma set Sad Horse Lady onto the table and sighed heavily. "I'm sorry, Otis. This game is really great, but I'm just too bummed out to play it right now."

"Hey," Otis said gently. "Don't worry about what happened tonight."

"*Pffft*," Thelma replied. "Yeah, right. You heard what those judges said. It's never gonna happen for us."

"No way, Thelma! We're just getting started. We'll have plenty of other chances." Otis began to gather up the pieces of his role-playing game.

Thelma shook her head, staring at the pitiful horse figurine that represented her character. "No. Everyone's always told me I didn't have the right looks for this. And you know what? I think they're right."

"Well, I think you're perfect," Otis said. He stood up from the table and shot his best friend a smile. "Good night, Thelma."

Chapter 7

When Thelma woke up the next morning, the unicorn figurine from the previous night's game was sitting on her nightstand. She sighed, immediately transported back to the memory of what had happened during their audition. Glumly, she got ready for work and set out for another ho-hum, totally ordinary day.

Thelma hauled a manure pile through the barnyard. Dumping it out at the edge of the pasture, she heard the flies cheering, "Yay! Breakfast!" as she headed back for more. To make things worse, just as she walked past the fence, the Rhinestone Fillies pranced past wearing their talent show medals.

"Group photo, everyone!" Claudia said, gathering

the three horses and her fellow human together for a photo shoot.

"We did it!" Esteban cheered.

"Rhinestone Fillies," Zirconia neighed. "Man, we killed that last night."

"Ew," Esteban said, moving slightly away from Zirconia's pink eye. "Move your eyeballs."

The group leaned in for a selfie. "Did we show up and show out?" Zirconia asked the others. "Yes, we did."

"That was amazing," Claudia sighed.

Zirconia tilted her head to one side just before they snapped the picture and said, "Hold on, now. Make sure you get my good eye."

Thelma wandered away, feeling even worse about herself than she had before. As she walked slowly across the pasture, she suddenly came upon a carrot that was just lying on the ground. She picked it up, considering its shape and size.

Next, she stuck the carrot on her head using mud and looked at her shadow on the ground. Her shadow looked like a unicorn! With a small smile, she posed and neighed, feeling just a little better than she had all day. She began to prance around, admiring her shadow, and owning the new character she'd become with just the tiniest shift in her appearance.

"Thelma?" Otis said, staring at his friend as she made unicorn noises and strutted around the pasture.

"Oh," Thelma said, only a little embarrassed. Friends understood you when you did things like pretend to be a unicorn. "Hey."

"Hey, weirdo," Otis said, grinning. "Nice carrot-horn."

"Otis, what do I remind you of?"

"Uh . . . a pony with a large, edible mass growing out of its brain?" Otis guessed.

"What?" Thelma wiggled the horn on her forehead. "No, you ding-dong. Come on, for real this time, try again."

While Otis considered the question, a delivery truck roared down the hill behind them. On the side of the truck were the words *GLITTER AND PAINT*, but Otis was too busy trying to guess Thelma's mystery character to notice.

"Wait!" Otis said. "I got it. You're a carrot with a pony stuck to its butt."

"Wrong! Come on, Otis, you can do better than that." She struck a pose as a noble unicorn, waiting for her friend to figure it out.

"Uhh . . ." Otis muttered. "Oh! You're the new mascot for Root Vegetable Awareness Month."

"Otis!" Thelma screeched. "You're killing me!"

Just then, the truck that had been barreling down the road beside them hit a pothole. It swerved off the road, bouncing wildly across the pasture—right toward Thelma and Otis! Otis was the first to see it. He screamed, "Watch out!"

Thelma spun around just in time to see the truck tip, and gallons of pink paint and glitter came soaring through the air. The pink sparkle rained down, covering Thelma from head to hoof.

"Ugh, gross!" Thelma said, blinking her eyes to clear them. "What is this stuff?"

"Uhh, Thelma?" Otis said, his eyes going wide as he got a good look at his buddy. "I think you better go take a look at yourself."

"I swear," Thelma muttered, shaking off some of the extra paint. "That dude needs to learn how to drive . . ." Thelma strolled over to a puddle and looked down at her reflection. "What?" Thelma gasped, realizing that she looked exactly like . . . a pink and sparkly unicorn! "I'm a unicorn . . . I'm a *unicorn*!"

Chapter 8

Thelma danced wildly, leaping and hopping off hay bales. This was the best day of her life—she was a unicorn!

"A *fake* unicorn," Otis pointed out.

"Who cares?" Thelma whooped. "Take a picture of me so I can post it on Picstagram!" She handed Otis her phone, then quickly grabbed it back. "Oh—wait, wait, wait. Let me delete my old account first. I'm gonna create a whole new profile. It'll be like the old me never existed!"

"Don't delete the old you!" Otis gasped. "I'm *friends* with the old you."

Thelma considered for just a second, then with a

click of a button—*poof!*—her old account was gone. "Yeah!"

"Are you kidding?" Otis asked.

"Here, just take the photo," Thelma urged. "Just take the photo!"

While Otis fooled around snapping pics of his unicorn-pal, a minivan rolled up beside the pasture. A little girl named Suzie poked her head out the window, then pointed. "Look, look! There's a unicorn! I told you they were real!"

Suzie's moms, Naomi and Maya, screamed joyfully along with their daughter and parked their car. Suzie rolled out of the car in a wheelchair, heading quickly toward Thelma. "Unicorn, unicorn, unicorn!"

Thelma waved to Suzie, while beside her, Otis leaned toward her to whisper, "So . . . you're just gonna let people think you're a real unicorn now?"

"Oh my gosh," Maya said, gazing at Thelma. "It's the best day of my life. She's so beautiful."

Thelma leaned toward her pal and said, "Well, I'm definitely not gonna break that little girl's heart." She trotted over to Suzie. "Hey, baby, what's your name?"

"Suzie," the little girl answered. "What's your name?"

"Thelma."

"Thelma the Unicorn?" Suzie squealed. "Can I take your picture?"

"Yeah, girl!" Thelma said, beaming. "Of *course* you can take my picture. But watch out, my sparkles might blow up your phone!"

Suzie giggled. While Naomi took photos from every angle, Maya asked, "Is this real, or is this a mirage?"

"I can't believe this," Naomi replied.

"What a dream duo," Maya noted. "Okay, get ready."

"Say cheese!" Naomi said. "Smile with them teeth!"

"Like this?" Suzie asked, grinning broadly.

"Too much teeth," Maya answered.

Suddenly, Suzie noticed that some of Thelma's fresh glitter had rubbed off onto her hand. "Unicorn dust?" she gasped. "I'll bet it tastes like candy!"

Thelma glanced up, noticing that at the edge of the pasture, a large crowd had gathered in the time she was taking pictures with Suzie. "I don't believe it!" a woman cried out, as Thelma lifted a hoof to wave. “A real unicorn?”

“I wonder if she can grant me eternal youth?” an old man asked hopefully.

“Can your horn shoot lasers?” another guy asked.

“Um . . .” Thelma wasn’t sure what the rules of unicorns were!

“Does your poop smell like flowers?” some kid asked.

“What color is your blood?” someone else shouted.

“Uh . . .” Thelma said. “Rainbow colored.”

“You don’t really sound like a unicorn,” a llama noted.

“Hey, what’s that supposed to mean?” Thelma asked.

The llama shrugged. “I thought they were supposed to sound like this.” The llama changed into a high, screeching baby voice and went on, *“Hi, I’m a unicorn! My tears turn into glitter and cupcakes.”*

“Yeah, well,” Thelma shrugged. “All those unicorns got eaten by dragons.”

“Can you do anything magical?” a guy called out.

“Magical?” Thelma asked. “Yeah, I can sing.”

The crowd began shouting, begging for Thelma to

sing for them. She was more than happy to do just that!

"Otis," Thelma whispered to her friend. "Go get your guitar! This is our big chance!"

"You can't be serious," Otis said. "You wanna perform like this?"

"Yes!" Thelma said. She noticed a little boy raising his hand and called on him.

"Um, excuse me," the little boy said shyly. "Are you really a real unicorn?"

Thelma took a moment to think. This was her opportunity to come clean—or it was her chance for a fresh start. "Yes," she said certainly. "Yes, I am." Otis shook his head, disappointed by her lie. But Thelma felt better than ever.

"Psst," Reggie said, appearing behind his two bandmates, instruments in hoof. "Thelma! The new makeover looks sick."

"Ugh," Otis said. "You gotta be kidding me."

Thelma glanced at her incredible reflection in the puddle again, blowing her bangs out of her face. Then, with a deep breath, she and the Rusty Buckets began to play.

Everyone watching went silent, in awe of Thelma's

voice. When Thelma finished her verse, the crowd went wild. She turned to Otis in disbelief. "Otis, I think they like it!"

"I know!" Otis said, finally grinning. "Keep going, keep going!"

Thelma sang on, feeling better than she ever had before in her life. The dream she had been waiting for her entire life was coming true right before her eyes. People were finally listening to her sing!

Suzie grabbed her phone and hit the live stream button. Within minutes, Thelma's song was being played on millions of phones and televisions all across the world—including one *very* important screen, in the living room of one of music's living legends: the one and only Peggy Purvis.

Peggy listened to Thelma crooning through the magic of live streaming. Peggy whistled in approval as Thelma kept singing.

Peggy's husband, Gerald, glanced over the top of his newspaper as his wife listened to Thelma's voice, tapping her white cane against the floor along with the beat, her eyebrows rising high above her dark sunglasses in surprise. The legendary Peggy Purvis was, for once, utterly speechless. He knew what it meant when Peggy reacted to music in the way she was at that very moment.

"Well," Gerald said, closing his newspaper. "Looks like we're going to see a unicorn."

Chapter 9

"I can't believe it, Otis," Thelma said after they'd bid their fans farewell and wrapped up the impromptu concert. "People actually liked our music."

"That was *awesome*," Otis agreed. He pointed at Thelma's paint and glitter. "But I think we should try to get this stuff off you now."

"What?" Thelma asked, stopping to stare at him. "No way. Nuh-uh, I'm not washing this off. This is exactly what I've been waiting for! I'm finally special."

Otis gaped at her. "You were special before all this, Thelma. You don't need this unicorn stuff—"

Thelma cut him off. "And why not? You pretend all the time. You're Dank-Poopy-Butt or whatever it is—"

"It's *Donk-Truvius,*" Otis clarified. "And that's totally different. That's just a game."

"But think about it, Otis," Thelma said. "No one even paid attention to us until I turned into this unicorn. The Rusty Buckets finally have a lead singer that looks like a star!"

Otis shrugged. "Yeah, but—I didn't think this would be a *forever* thing."

"Come on," Thelma said. "People are finally giving our music a chance." She made pony eyes at him, begging him to go along with this idea. If being a unicorn was the only thing she needed to do to get people to notice their music, then that's what she would do!

Otis grumbled, "Ugh, fine."

Thelma's phone dinged, and she pulled it out. She thrust it into Otis's face and said, "Otis! Look! Yeahhh!"

Even Otis couldn't resist a smile when he saw the video of them, the Rusty Buckets, going viral. People really did love them . . . finally!

Chapter 10

Meanwhile, outside Nikki Narwhal's mansion, no one had yet realized there was a new star—Thelma the Unicorn!—that was about to explode into the music world. Deepak, one of Nikki's Pool Boys was dancing around the mansion's courtyard with a bucket of cod and a boom box. It was time to get the party started! Dante sprayed everyone with a hose, which made all the other Pool Boys laugh.

"Pool Boys!" yelled Megan, Nikki's human super-fan turned assistant. "What the heck are you doing?" The Pool Boys all hung their heads, ashamed. "I already done told y'all," Megan continued. "No more dillydallying around the veranda."

Suddenly, Nikki breached the pool's surface, thoroughly soaking Megan and the Pool Boys. "Hey, hey, you guys! Ba-bam! Guess who's back in the house!" The Pool Boys all beamed at her. Megan looked like a drowned rat. "Good morning, Megan. How's my favorite little assistant?"

Megan grinned at her, even though she was soaking wet. "Doing great, Nikki."

"Get in here, boys," Nikki called out to her posse. "The water's great."

While the Pool Boys goofed off and played games in the water around Nikki the Narwhal, Megan went over Nikki's schedule with her. "So, you've got a photo shoot at noon, a blubber massage at one, and . . . you are getting a seaweed colonic at three."

"Ugh," Nikki moaned.

"Hey, Nikki!" Vic Diamond, her manager, called out from the balcony overlooking the pool. "What a morning!" Dropping his robe, Vic leapt off the balcony and dove into the pool. After a quick lap, he hopped out, dried himself off, and changed into the day's jumpsuit. Then he settled in at the breakfast table with a newspaper. "Oh, baby . . ." he said, scanning the headline. It read, "Queen of Pop, or Queen of Flop?"

He glanced at Nikki, who was still relaxing in the pool, and said, "Nikki, there's an *awful* review of your show in the paper. I don't want you to hear it at all. Listen." After just a momentary pause, Vic immediately began to read it aloud. "'A bloated whale carcass was discovered in Las Vegas Friday night, three hundred miles from the nearest beach. It was Nikki Narwhal, whose new show has the smell of low tide.'" Vic looked up and cringed. "Oh, ouchie."

Nikki lounged in the pool and asked, "Vic, why are you reading this to me?"

"Yeah, Vic," Megan chirped. "What the heck?"

Vic shrugged. "Well, because I'm your manager, darling."

Nikki burst out of the water, getting right up in Vic's face. "I don't care what the critics say! My fans love 'Blubber Trouble'! It's the number one song in the world right now."

Megan held out her hand, showing Vic the latest music chart to prove it. Megan glanced at her phone, then quietly said, "You're right, Nikki. Number one, but with a two after it."

Nikki slumped back into the pool as Vic said, "Nikki, I'm going to tell ya like it is, because I love ya.

Your fame is on life support. If we don't find some kind of a jolt soon, your career will be dead as a dodo."

"Well, fix it, then!" Nikki ordered.

"We need to build your brand beyond music, Nikki," Vic explained. "We need to strategize."

The Pool Boys hoisted Nikki out of the pool using a large crane. She glared at Vic and said, "You're the manager. *You* strategize." She turned to her assistant and said, "Megan, get me a bucket of cod—now!"

"You got it, girlfriend," Megan said. She trailed after her boss while holding a bucket of slimy cod. "Later, Vic," she called out over her shoulder.

But Vic didn't hear her—because he was busy staring at his phone, watching Thelma's viral video. The banner on-screen called out "Singing Unicorn Goes Viral." Vic grinned as he watched the video, already seeing stars in his eyes.

Chapter 11

Later that night, back on the farm, Thelma and Otis were playing Dungeons & Wagons on a makeshift table.

"Uh-oh," Otis said when Thelma rolled her dice. "That's not good. You just summoned a demon." Otis held out a demon figurine and shook it in front of her face.

"Oh, yeah?" Thelma blurted. "Well, bring it on, demon!" She clashed her figurine into Otis's demon, and the two battled it out.

Eventually, Otis's demon took Thelma's horse down. "No!" Thelma wailed. "You've taken my soul!"

She dropped her face onto the table but picked it up again just as quickly when she heard music playing somewhere off in the distance. "Hold up. Do you hear that?"

"Uh, yeah," Otis said.

Thelma and Otis stepped away from the game table to find the source of the sound. All the way across the farm, there was a vintage car parked near their rehearsal shed. Exchanging curious looks, they headed that way and poked their heads inside the shed. There was Reggie—and he was jamming with someone.

"Whoa," Otis said, staring at the middle-aged woman wearing dark sunglasses who was rocking out on the guitar. "Is that—"

Thelma's face lit up when she realized who it was. "That's—that's Peggy Purvis! The legendary music producer!"

"No way," Otis said. "I thought she retired."

"What is she doing here?" Thelma wondered.

Peggy's husband, Gerald, stepped over to Thelma. "I believe she's here to see you, little missy."

"Whoa . . ." Thelma said. This was too much. Impossible. But also . . . happening?

Just then, Peggy and Reggie wrapped up their jam session. "Oh, those were some stanky licks," Reggie said, nodding at Peggy.

Peggy laughed. "You're pretty stanky yourself," she told Reggie.

"Woo-hoo!" Thelma cheered. "That sounded amazing, y'all."

Reggie hopped off the stage and rushed over to Thelma. "Thelma! Thelma! Thelma! I just got to jam with a guitar legend!"

"I know," Thelma said, laughing. "That's so cool!"

Peggy walked in Thelma's direction, using a white cane to help guide her. "Thelma, right?" she asked. "I'm Peggy Purvis."

"Wow," Thelma said. "I'm a huge fan."

Peggy smiled. "Well . . . that song you sang on the news today—I ain't never heard anything like it."

"For real?" Thelma asked. "Thank you!"

"How'd you come up with it?" Peggy asked.

"Oh, that old thing?" Thelma said. "I wrote that song a long time ago. I've just never had a chance to play it for anybody."

"Gee, kid," Peggy said, leaning on her cane. "You're really somethin' special."

"And she's a unicorn!" Reggie blurted out.

"Ha!" Peggy laughed. "I don't care what she is. This girl, she could sing the phone book and make you cry."

"I don't know about that," Thelma said.

Peggy got right to the point and said, "So . . . you kids wanna make a record?"

Reggie and Otis screamed silently, while Thelma was struck speechless. This was a dream come true! She began to dance, still unable to utter a single word.

"Babe?" Peggy said to Gerald. "Are they alright?"

"They're fine, sweetheart," Gerald assured her. "They're all just kinda doing this weird silent dance."

"Are you serious?!" Thelma blurted out, snapping out of her silence. "That would be our dream. But I thought you, uh . . ."

"Stopped producing music after I went blind?" Peggy broke in. "Yeah, well, maybe *you* can be my comeback." Thelma smiled and gasped. Then Peggy turned and strode out of the barn, calling over her shoulder, "Grab your bags. I'm not getting any younger."

Otis freaked out as soon as Peggy and Gerald had stepped outside. "We're making an album with *Peggy Purvis*?" he screamed. *"Whaaaaat?!"*

Chapter 12

"Watch your step," Peggy said, leading Thelma, Otis, and Reggie into the recording booth at Rawhide Records. The Rusty Buckets all looked around, starstruck, as they took in the walls covered in gold records and pictures of Peggy from early in her career.

"Wow," Thelma said. "I've never been in a real studio before."

"Well, get used to it," Peggy said with a chuckle. "My gut tells me you're gonna be in here a lot."

Thelma spotted a picture of Patsy Swine and Smokey Buffalo on the wall. "No way!" she said. "You recorded Patsy Swine and Smokey Buffalo here?"

Peggy strode over toward Thelma. "Sure did. And

someday, the Rusty Buckets' picture is gonna be up there, too." She hip-bumped Thelma. "Boom!" Then she jumped into a chair across from Thelma and picked up her guitar.

While Peggy tuned her instrument, Thelma settled onto a stool. "Ya know, it's funny—a lot of people told us we'd never make it 'cause we didn't look like stars."

"It's a good thing I don't care what you look like, Thelma," Peggy said.

Thelma smiled and then asked, "Peggy, be real with me: Do you think you can get us into Sparkle-Palooza?"

"Nope," Peggy said. "I can't guarantee anything like that." Before Thelma could respond, Peggy went on, "But *you* can get yourself to Sparkle-Palooza by singing the truth, singing from your heart." She handed Thelma the guitar.

"Yeah," Thelma said, carefully taking the instrument into her hooves. "I've got this one song I've been working on since I was a little kid. I've just never found the right words for it."

Peggy shrugged. "Don't worry, baby. Lyrics are like food poisoning: It hits ya when you least expect it." As Thelma laughed, Peggy added, "Now show me what you got cookin' in that songbook of yours. It's time to jam!"

Chapter 13

A few days later, after a successful jam session, Peggy, Gerald, and the band were relaxing and hanging out, when Gerald thrust his phone toward Peggy and said, "Honey, I think you better take this."

Peggy took the phone and held it up to her ear. "Peggy, darling!" Vic Diamond crooned through the phone. "I've got great news for you. Listen, I'm so glad you answered, because I thought you'd probably be dead by now. Hey, I'm delighted to be wrong this time!"

"What do you want, Vic?" Peggy said, annoyed. She couldn't stand Vic—the famous music manager just couldn't be trusted.

"Well, buckle up, Peggy," Vic said, using his most charming voice. "I've called to make you and that singing unicorn an offer." He paused. "An offer you cannot refuse."

"Oh, yes, I can. Check this out." Peggy put her mouth close to the phone and said confidently, "Offer refused!"

"Oh, well, I suppose you're not interested in her opening for Nikki Narwhal today at her live show?" Vic asked.

"Not gonna happen, Vic."

"Come on, Peggy," Vic urged. "I don't have time for patty-cake. I don't have the cake, and you know darn well I don't have the patties. You wouldn't want to be the only one standing in the way of her success, would you?"

Peggy considered this. It *was* a great offer for Thelma and the Rusty Buckets. She sighed.

"What?" Thelma asked her. "What is it?"

"You kids wanna open for Nikki Narwhal this afternoon?" Peggy asked.

"What?" Thelma screamed. "Are you serious?"

"I dunno, Thelma," Otis cut in. "I don't think we're ready for a big stage like that."

"What are you talking about?" Thelma said. "This is a huge opportunity!"

Otis leaned in to whisper, "I know we've already talked about this, but don't you want to wash the paint off first?"

Whispering back, Thelma answered, "No way, man. I ain't gonna mess this up. It'll ruin everything!" She turned to Peggy and made a final decision on behalf of the band. "Peggy, we'll do it! *Ahhhh!*"

Chapter 14

Not long after Peggy had taken Vic's call, she and the Rusty Buckets waited on the tarmac at the airport. They all watched as a giant airplane, shaped just like Nikki Narwhal herself, began its descent. That was the plane coming to pick them up!

As soon as it landed, workers pushed a staircase up to the plane door and Vic Diamond stepped out. Thelma watched in awe as he changed from eyeglasses to sunglasses and began to dance. "Peggy, darling," Vic crooned as he landed in the splits. "Looking great! Did you just buy your clothes at a rodeo? Yeehaw!"

Peggy raised her cane, the tip aimed at Vic's face,

silencing him. "Vic," she said levelly. "Still rockin' that handsome smile. Good for you!"

Vic swatted her away, then belly flopped onto the ground, right in front of Thelma. "Oh, baby! Look at you, you're a star! Like a fluffy piece of cotton candy with legs!"

Thelma shrugged. "Yeah, well, I'm nothing without my band."

"Vicky D," Reggie whooped. "What up?"

Vic grimaced as he took in Reggie and Otis. "Oh, hello, donkey boys." Vic shifted his attention back to Thelma. "Hey, look! I bought us some matching diamond bracelets." He snapped one onto his wrist. "And wowee, they're connected!" Thelma looked down as Vic made a move to put the other on her wrist. She realized that the bracelets were, in fact, connected to each other by a chain.

"Uh . . ." Otis said, weirded out.

"Okay . . ." Reggie mused.

Vic laughed as he latched the other bracelet onto Thelma. But before he could clip it into place, Peggy stepped forward and blocked Vic with her cane again. "Come on, child. Let's go." She placed her hand on Thelma's back, and gently guided her toward the waiting plane and away from Vic's chains.

Otis and Reggie trailed behind, feeling a little uncomfortable, but once the group was airborne, their excitement began to creep back in. By the time they landed in Vegas, Reggie couldn't contain his enthusiasm. "Yeah!" he cheered, as the dancing Pool Boys led the group toward two stretch limos.

"Wow," Thelma said, watching the Pool Boys with a smile. "Those dudes sure like to dance."

"These are the Pool Boys," Vic explained. "They say if they stop dancing, they die." He ushered Thelma into the first limo. "Right this way—unicorns first!"

"Wow!" Thelma said.

Vic nodded to the Pool Boys, who quickly ushered Peggy, Otis, and Reggie into the other limo. "Oh, I think they want us to go in *that* limo," Reggie said, glancing over at Thelma—who was climbing into the other limo without them.

Otis looked on disappointedly as Thelma waved goodbye. "See you guys at the hotel!"

"Last one there is a smelly donkey," Vic said with a smirk and a knowing wink. "Ta-ta!"

Thelma was captivated as she and Vic rode through

the Vegas Strip. She stuck her head out of the limo and took in all the sights. It was incredible!

"Look!" Vic said, pointing. "It's your name in lights!"

Sure enough, a giant billboard read:

NIKKI TONIGHT! INTRODUCING:

Thelma the Unicorn!

While Thelma was distracted, staring at her own name on a marquee, Vic quietly and carefully pressed a secret red button on his watch. Moments later, the license plate on their limo popped open and a robot arm emerged to deploy a small missile in the direction of the other limo.

The limo carrying Otis, Reggie, and Peggy was hit by the missile and quickly sputtered to a stop.

"Oh, man, what just happened?" Otis asked.

Reggie watched in shock as the limo carrying their friend Thelma zipped away. "Bummer."

Chapter 15

Inside Nikki Narwhal's dressing room, things were getting tense. "I don't know why Vic thinks I need some stupid unicorn to sell tickets to my own show!" she ranted to Megan. "I've never needed an opening act!"

Megan nodded. "That pink unicorn's got nothing on you. Now hit me with that freestyle!"

Nikki held her flipper up to her ear cavity and sang out, "I'm a whale that sings. I'm a whale that sings really well. I'm a better swimmer than you 'cause you got four legs and I got a tail." Nikki was startled into silence when there was a loud knock on her dressing room door.

"Oh, Nikki, darling," Vic Diamond said, sweeping into the room with Thelma at his heels, trying to keep up. "Megan." He nodded at Nikki's assistant, who'd been soaked by yet another blast from Nikki's blowhole. "This little honey horse is Thelma the Unicorn. She's a big, yet minuscule, fan."

"Heyyy," Thelma said, trying to act cool. Nikki and Megan both gave her a once-over, then turned away without a word.

"Oh, Nikki," Vic said, shaking his head. "You're so awkward."

The rest of the day was all about getting ready for the show. When showtime rolled around, Thelma snuck a peek from her hiding spot backstage and saw that it was a totally packed house. Moments later, she heard the announcer say, "Opening today, performing for the first time ever, we bring you the viral singing sensation, Thelma the Unicorn!"

Thelma looked around desperately. Where were Otis and Reggie? She hadn't seen either of them since the group left the airport earlier in the day. It was go time! "Vic!" she yelled. "I can't do this without my band. Where are they?"

Vic gasped. "Oh no, do you think they've abandoned you?"

"No!" Thelma said quickly. "Of course not."

Vic shrugged. "Some bands just aren't ready for the big stage."

"But they wouldn't just bail like that . . ." Thelma said. She knew her friends, and she knew they wouldn't skip this without telling her.

"You poor, poor thing," Vic soothed her. "I know how badly you wanted this." He knelt down so he and Thelma were face-to-face. "Would you like me to cancel the show?"

Thelma considered this. After a moment's thought, she said, "No. I've been waiting for something like this my whole life. Let's do this thing."

"Fantastic!" Vic cheered. "Now get out there and show everyone how special you are!"

She took a deep breath and stepped out onto the stage. "Hi, everybody," she said into the mic. "I'm Thelma the Unicorn."

The crowd went wild as soon as Thelma kicked off her set. "When the world's so big," she began to croon, "it's easy to feel small. When no one's ever looking down, no, nobody sees me and nobody wants to be me." Thelma reveled in the crowd's attention as she continued to sing. "I'm gonna have to show 'em now. I'm fresh out of chances left untaken. Gonna work on my moves, baby, I've been makin' . . ."

"We love you, Thelma!" the crowd screamed.

"And I'm done shrinking to fit into spaces," Thelma belted. "It's time to show the world that I am going places!"

Suzie, the little girl who had first filmed Thelma's performance, reached up for a high five from her favorite unicorn.

As she strutted through the crowd, Thelma flashed Suzie a smile. "Go big or go home," she sang. "If you fall, dust it off and get back on your feet. You gotta go big or go home. Leave my things at the door, 'cause there's no one like me."

Meanwhile, outside the concert venue, Otis, Reggie, and Peggy were desperately trying to reach Thelma in time for their show. As they raced up to the front doors of the hotel, they were stopped by security guards. "Hey, hey! Hold it right there!"

"But we're supposed to be opening for Nikki!" Otis explained.

"Uh," the security guard said, tilting his head to one side. "Well, you guys showed up way too late." He pointed to a monitor, where Thelma's live performance was being streamed.

Thelma's two best friends watched, standing alongside Peggy as Thelma sang, "I'm fresh out of chances left untaken. Gonna work on my moves, baby—I've been making. I'm done shrinking to fit into spaces. It's time to show the world what I've been making. You gotta go big or go home. If you fall, dust it off and get back on your feet."

Otis and Reggie couldn't believe it. Had Thelma gone onstage . . . without them?

Backstage, Vic stepped toward a control panel to set off a round of fireworks onstage. The whole scene was magical, but there was one star that didn't appreciate the show. Nikki Narwhal had seen enough. She shot water through her blowhole, totally soaking her assistant.

"Vic!" Megan yelled, sensing her boss's rotten mood. "What are you doin'?" She stomped over to Vic, hands on her hips. "Those fireworks were for Nikki!"

Vic tapped at Megan's phone to show her that Thelma's performance was seriously trending. He smirked and said, "It appears that Vic Diamond has just given birth to a new diamond." He shredded Nikki's contract and announced, "Good luck finding a new manager, Nikki. Because we're through."

Chapter 16

When she'd finished her performance, Thelma basked in the crowd's applause. "Thank you! Thank you so much!" The crowd continued to applaud while Thelma soaked it all in.

But then, suddenly, Nikki crashed through the curtain wearing a wire harness. "Get! Off! My! Stage!" she bellowed.

"Yeah," Megan cheered, as Nikki swung recklessly through the air, back and forth across the stage. "Beat her butt!"

"Nikki, no!" Thelma begged as Nikki swung dangerously out over the audience. "Please, please, please!" But it was no use. A swinging Nikki crashed into a panel of stage lights, laughing as sparks flew out in every direction.

"DJ!" Nikki screamed. "Play my music!"

The DJ immediately cranked on "Blubber Trouble." Her Pool Boys danced and swayed onstage as Nikki sang loudly to try to cover up the sounds of the booing crowd. Nikki continued to sing even as a chant of "Unicorn! Unicorn! Unicorn!" roared up from the crowd.

The whole scene was too much, even for someone as tough and confident as Nikki Narwhal. As she swung recklessly over the stage, her tusk shredded a huge hole into the floor—and then Nikki went plummeting into it.

"I got you, girl!" Megan called, diving in after her boss. They were both gone.

Backstage, Thelma couldn't believe all the trouble she'd caused. "I'm so sorry, Vic," she said. "I didn't mean for this to happen."

Vic shrugged. "Once a star goes supernova, a *new* star can take its place. I could turn you into the biggest star on the planet, Thelma."

"Thanks, Vic," Thelma said. "But I've already got Peggy to help with my music."

Vic leaned down and said quietly, "Thelma, Thelma . . . If you stay with Peggy, you'll *never* make it to Sparkle-Palooza." He grinned his five-hundred-watt grin. "Don't you get it? Working with me will *guarantee* that you play there someday."

"Well," Thelma said, considering this. "Can I bring my band with me?"

Vic threw his hands up in the air. "Of course you can, darling!" He pulled out a sheet of paper and a pen, sliding them in front of Thelma's snout. "Sign with me, and your dream will become a reality." He nodded toward the crowd, who were still chanting Thelma's name. "I'm only going to make this offer once."

Thelma looked out at the packed house. Vic was making things happen—he knew how to make a star. Maybe it was worth considering his offer. She thought for another moment, then grabbed Vic's pen and signed.

"Congratulations, my dear unicorn," Vic said with a sly sparkle in his eye. "We are officially in business."

Chapter 17

That evening, Vic and Thelma stepped out onto the rooftop helipad at their hotel and were immediately greeted by paparazzi and fans.

One trio of fans—Garyl, Cheryl, and Beryl—had already declared themselves to be Thelma's biggest fans. "Thelma!" Garyl called out, waving sheets of paper in her direction. "I have these adoption papers that will legally make me your son! Will you sign them for me?"

Distracted by all the newfound attention, Thelma took the papers in hand and signed them. No one had ever asked for her autograph before!

"Look!" Vic said, pointing up into the sky. "Your very own Uni-Chopper!"

A helicopter floated down from the sky just as Thelma heard a familiar voice calling her name from across the rooftop. "Thelma!" Otis cried. Thelma spun around, searching for her friends in the crowd. Otis shook off a security guard, blurting out, "Hey, let go of me!"

"Otis!" Thelma said, shouting to be heard over the noise of the helicopter. "Where have you been?"

"We've been trying to find *you*," Otis said. "Why did you perform without us?"

"What was I supposed to do? You guys completely abandoned me," Thelma reminded them.

"We didn't abandon you!" Otis yelled. "A missile came out of nowhere and blew up our car!"

"C'mon, Otis," Thelma said, shaking her head. "You don't have to make up stories. Just tell me the truth."

"I'm serious," Otis insisted. That was exactly what had happened—it's just that no one knew that was what had actually happened.

"Look," Thelma said sadly. "I don't wanna fight with you. Vic promised me he could get us all to Sparkle-Palooza, so let's go."

"I knew this unicorn stuff would go to your head," Otis grumbled.

"Gimme a break," Thelma said, taking a deep breath and raising her voice so her friend could hear her over the noise of the chopper. "You didn't even wanna be here! You said we weren't ready for the big stage."

"Mommy," Garyl the fan said, sidling up beside Thelma. "Is this donkey bothering you?"

"Hey, hold on," Otis said, gesturing to Garyl. "Who is this?"

"I am her son," Garyl said simply.

"Your *son*?" Otis asked.

"Yeah," Garyl spat. "Go away!"

Otis glared at Thelma. "You're just going to let your son talk to me like that?"

"Otis," Thelma said, ignoring his question. "I've been wanting this my whole life. I'm tired of being overlooked."

"If you've been wanting this your whole life," Otis said, "then why are you screwing it up by pretending to be someone else?"

Thelma hung her head. That stung. She gave her friend one last, sad look and then spun and walked away from him.

As the crowd of fans swallowed up his best friend, Otis was stunned. What had just happened?

"Hey, Thelma, over here!" a paparazzo shouted. "Smile for the cameras!"

The crowd caught up with Otis, but he barely noticed. He was too busy watching, speechless, as Thelma stepped up onto the uni-chopper with Vic Diamond.

"We love you!" Garyl called after her.

Heartbroken, all Otis could do was stare.

Chapter 18

Nikki Narwhal was furious. All evening long, she'd been watching news coverage of that afternoon's performance. While she soaked in her hot tub and tried to relax, she was drawn out of her zen by a reporter's harsh words: "Will Nikki Narwhal ever bounce back from her epic meltdown? Or is it the end of the road for this disgraced diva?" Nikki glared at the screen, watching mobs of people ducking for cover as they replayed her onstage Thelma attack from earlier that day. The news reporter shook her head sadly onscreen and finished up. "Look out, Nikki, 'cause you're about to get replaced by Thelma the Uni—"

Before the newscaster could finish her sentence,

Nikki slashed her tusk through the TV screen, silencing the report. She slumped down in her hot tub. Nearby, Megan was trying hard to cheer up her boss by tossing some tasty cod nibbles into the air.

"Listen, Megan," Nikki said, catching a chunk of cod in her gaping mouth. "Listen a lot. The only way I'll ever be back on top is if we *destroy* Thelma."

"Ooh!" Megan said, clapping. "Are we talking about murder here?"

"What?" Nikki asked, snapping another fish chunk out of the air. "No! I just need you to dig up the dirt that will ruin her forever . . . because everyone's got secrets."

Megan grinned. "Oh *wow.* You are so dang smart, Nikki. I swear, it's that big ole whale brain of yours!"

"Well, thank you," Nikki preened. "My doctor says it's mainly water." She and Megan cracked up.

Still giggling madly, Megan said, "Boom, Nikki! You go, girl!"

Nikki stopped laughing and looked pointedly at her assistant. "Well, what are you waiting for? Get out there and find that unicorn's dirty little secrets."

"Oh, yeah," Megan said. She tossed one last fish into the air for Nikki, then hightailed it out into the world to dig up some unicorn dirt.

Chapter 19

Thelma had never seen anything like Vic Diamond's penthouse. It filled the uppermost floor of an entire building that belonged to Vic. But even surrounded by Vic's vast riches and fancy digs, all Thelma could look at was a picture of her band. She sure did miss the guys.

"Boom, sha-bang!" Vic said, thundering into the room holding a bucket. "Good morning, my little pink glitter puff! I've brought you some noodles and candies."

"Um," Thelma said, glancing into the bucket that was, in fact, filled with noodles and candy.

"I don't know what unicorns eat," Vic explained. "Is it noodles and candies?"

Thelma pushed the bucket aside and said, "Vic, I think I've made a huge mistake."

"Oh no!" Vic said, flopping down beside her. "What is it, my love?"

"I shouldn't have left my band and Peggy like that," Thelma said.

"Aw, come, come," Vic said. "That ship has sailed, darling." He thrust his face in front of Thelma's. "But don't you worry! Because we're going to make some sweet unicorn magic together."

Thelma took a deep breath. "There's something I've got to tell you first."

"Yes?" Vic said, urging her to go on.

"I'm . . ." Thelma gulped. "Not a real unicorn." She swiped some of the paint off her body, revealing her real fur beneath the pink shimmer.

Vic gasped. "No! Please tell me you're joking." He paused, then shook his head. "Oh, wait. I don't care."

"You don't?" Thelma asked, surprised.

"Of course not!" Vic said. He grinned at her and added, "You think these teeth are real?" He reached into his mouth and pulled out his fake set of giant, gnarled teeth and then grinned again—to reveal a full set of tiny nubby teeth.

"Ahh!" Thelma gasped, horrified at the baby teeth inside Vic's mouth.

"Truth is the death of success," Vic pointed out. He popped his giant teeth back in, then added, "The most important thing in the music biz is how you look." He stood up, leaving Thelma to think about what he'd said. "Why don't you chew on that knowledge bomb and see how it tastes . . ."

Thelma nodded. "Alright, then." She exhaled deeply. "Tell me what I gotta do."

"That's my unicorn!" Vic whooped. He walked over to his record player and pulled out a record. "You're lucky, because I'm going to teach you what I taught *me* a long time ago—*The Three Cs to Success.*" He held up the record, showing Thelma that it was a self-help album.

Music began to play as Vic continued his lesson in song form. "Step one: *Change.* To be successful you have to change—not once, but every day, sometimes twice a day."

Vic snapped his fingers and a flurry of assistants wheeled in racks of clothing, makeup, wigs, fake teeth, and jewelry. "But I'm already a unicorn," Thelma pointed out.

Vic continued to sing as his assistants transformed Thelma into a series of different looks.

He showed Thelma a picture of herself in one of the new outfits, and Thelma gasped. "That doesn't look like me!"

Vic just grinned, unbothered. He led Thelma out of the penthouse and into his speed boat, singing the whole way.

For the next part of his lesson, Vic takes Thelma to a perfume factory, pulling her into a giant lab filled with scents and potions. "Step two: Cologne," he explained.

"What?" Thelma asked, baffled by how her smell was relevant to her success.

"Perfume, eau de toilette, whiffy stuff," Vic explained. "The nose jollies, darling."

"Do I smell bad or something?" Thelma asked, subtly sniffing herself to check.

Vic booped Thelma on the nose. A scientist tickled Thelma's nose with a feather, which made her sneeze. They caught her sneeze droplets in a petri dish, then ran the sample through a machine.

The machine spit out a bottle of something, which Thelma noticed was labeled *UNICORNIA N°5*. Vic sprayed it into Thelma's face, making her cough in disgust. It smelled terrible!

Thelma could do nothing but listen as Vic continued to sing, neither noticing that the scientist lurking next to them was none other than Megan.

Before Vic got to step three, he paused, growing somber as he told Thelma that he too had once been a nobody. He knew how hard it was to be rejected over and over again.

Thelma was surprised to hear that Vic, too, had once been a nobody who wanted to be somebody.

Vic stopped singing and explained, "That's when I changed my name from Dick Cumbersome to Vic Diamond; I became a mover and shaker; I became the star maker!" He shook his head to clear away the memories of what *was* and came back to the project currently in front of him—Thelma. "But I digress," he sang. "Back to my Three Cs of Success. The third *C*: Partnership!"

"But that don't start with a *C*," Thelma pointed out.

"Nobody interrupts Vic Diamond except Vic Diamond!" Vic growled.

"My bad . . ." Thelma apologized.

Leaving the perfume factory, Vic pulled Thelma

down the street, heading for the Hollywood Walk of Fame.

He wrapped his arm through Thelma's, then sang on as they traipsed through Hollywood.

After frolicking through the city, Vic ushered Thelma back to his car. The Three Cs to Success was stuck in Thelma's head as Vic drove her back to her all-celebrity hotel.

Chapter 20

"So, what's the plan now?" Thelma asked, as she and Vic collapsed onto sofas in the hotel lobby.

"I'm so glad you asked," Vic replied. "See that handsome stud over there?" He pointed at a horse with a long blond mane that was sitting across the room. "That's Danny Stallion, Video Tube Tube megastar!"

Thelma watched as Danny Stallion blew his bangs out of his eyes and greeted a fan. "Hey, nice to meet you," Danny said to the fan in a very charming voice.

"No way," Thelma said, realizing what Vic was up to. "Nuh-uh, I do *not* want a fake boyfriend!"

"He got famous last year for his cud-chewing videos," Vic said, ignoring Thelma's declaration altogether. He passed her his phone, which was playing a video of Danny chomping some cabbage—fortunately, it cut out before the video got to the part where Danny spewed the cud out.

"Ugh, nasty," Thelma said. "He got famous for that?"

Vic nodded. "Over a billion views and counting. Now get over there and make some sparks fly for the cameras!"

"What?" Thelma asked, as Vic gave her a gentle nudge in Danny's direction.

"Give love a chance!" Vic urged.

Thelma sighed. "Ugh, alright—you're the star maker."

Vic cheered. "Off we go! This is happening!" He shooed her over to Danny's table, where she plunked down into the seat across from the famous horse.

"Uh, you must be Danny," Thelma said awkwardly.

"Hey, you must be Thelma," Danny replied in his smooth voice. Clearly, he'd been expecting her—that Vic was sneaky. He'd obviously been planning this whole meetup all along! "You wanna see something cool?"

Thelma did not. "Uh, no, I'm good."

Danny leaned across the table and whispered, "Hey, aren't you gonna play along? There are people watching us—"

Thelma cut him off—suddenly, he sounded very different than he had a moment ago. "Whoa, what happened to your voice?"

"C'mon," Danny said with a shrug. "*You* know. This whole thing is just an act. I'm actually studying to be a brain surgeon."

"You are?" Thelma gasped. This was a surprise—was *everyone* pretending to be someone they weren't?

"Gotta pay for med school somehow, right?" Danny whispered. "Now let's give the people what they want!"

"Okay," Thelma agreed, just as Danny leaned in and burped in her face.

"Uh-oh," he brayed loudly. "Here comes the cud!" With a retching motion for effect, Danny leaned forward and regurgitated food came shooting out of his nostrils.

Thelma was mortified—but the fans who'd spotted them in the hotel's lobby were eating it up. "Woo! Yeah!" They cheered. "Yeah, Danny! Danny is the coolest!"

Danny chuckled. "Heh heh . . ."

“Danny and Thelma!” someone called, waving their arm. “Over here!” Thelma glanced over and noticed that a crowd of paparazzi had gathered outside the hotel’s front window.

“Hey, lovebirds,” one of them cried out. “Quick smiles for the camera!”

Danny pulled Thelma in close, but Thelma still wasn’t used to all the attention. It was clear she was going to have to *get* used to it, right quick.

Chapter 21

While Thelma and Danny Stallion got to know each other better, Otis was hanging out at Peggy's, playing a solo game of Dungeons & Wagons. "Ever since Sad Horse Lady left my side," he said to himself, slumping sadly over his figurines, "the goblins have laid siege to the Oregon Trail. Will life on the prairie ever be the same?"

He launched a fireball toward the wagon train, then moved his figurines around the table. Missing Thelma, he picked up a barbarian figurine and made it speak in a Thelma-like voice. "Donk-Truvius, look out!" he said, moving the barbarian Thelma figurine into position to bash an attacking goblin. "Leaving you was a huge mistake, Donk-Truvius," Otis said in his Thelma voice. "Let's get the band back together and join forces, posthaste!"

"That's a splendid idea," Otis said in his Donk-Truvius voice.

Reggie and Peggy wandered into the studio just in time to hear Otis's role-play exchange. "Too late for that, bro," Reggie muttered. Otis scrambled to hide his figurines before they realized he was playing a game by himself. Reggie went on, "Looks like Thelma's already got a new bandmate." He leaned in to show Otis a news report on his phone. In it was a picture of Thelma and Danny sneaking out of a tattoo parlor.

On-screen, the newscaster's voice reported, "The hot new couple—now known as 'Dannelma'—went public today by announcing a whole new line of game-changing products." Otis continued to watch, cringing as Danny wrapped his arm around Thelma.

"Don't forget to try our new cereal," Thelma said to the cameras, pulling out a box of cereal with her and Danny's faces on it. "Thelm-o's and D-Flakes! Yummy yum. And as a special prize, I've hidden five unicorn hairs inside each box!"

"I'm really sorry, boys," Peggy said.

Otis tossed the phone back to Reggie. It looked like the Rusty Buckets were officially over.

Chapter 22

"Right this way, watch your step," Vic Diamond said, ushering Thelma and Danny into the studio at Sellout Records. "This is my inner sanctum, where all the magic happens. Can you smell the success? That's my cologne."

Danny laughed. "Cool."

"Uh," Thelma said, looking around. "Where are your instruments?"

"Oh, Thelma," Vic said with a laugh. He led them to a recording booth and explained, "This is the auto-tune room. I suspect you'll be spending a lot of time in here, Danny."

"Awesome," Danny cheered in his cheesy celebrity voice.

Thelma rolled her eyes. "You can drop the act, buddy. There's nobody here to impress."

Danny slipped back into his normal voice to say, "Sorry. Sometimes I think the character I've created might actually be the real me."

"Oh boy," Thelma said.

Vic led the pair into another room, this one with a giant computer. "This is our lyrics room," he said, pointing at the computer. "And that's Bridget, the AI machine that generates all the hits." He waggled his eyebrows at Danny and Thelma. "Any ideas for a song, you two?"

"Oh yeah!" Thelma said eagerly. "I got a song idea right here. I just need some lyrics for it." She pulled out her songbook but didn't open it when she saw Vic's expression.

"No, no, no, no," he said. "We're not making *your* music, you silly goose. The algorithm will give us the groove!"

"What are you talking about?" Thelma asked, confused. "I got a book full of jams ready to go right now. We just gotta go in there and lay 'em down."

Danny broke in, "How 'bout we make a song about my cud?"

Thelma leveled him with a stare. "Are you for real?"

"Excellent idea, Danny Stallion," Vic said, turning to the computer. "Bridget, give me a song about the partly digested food particles known as *cud*."

"Anything for you, Vic," the computer replied. A second later, the printer spit out a piece of paper with song lyrics.

"Nice one, Bridget," Vic said, scanning the page. He handed the lyric sheet to Danny and said, "Get ready, you two. We're about to shake the world!"

Thelma soon found out that "shake the world" meant film a music video about cud on a yacht. Thelma tried not to look too disturbed when Danny, wearing a chain that said *Cud Life*, began to sing "Here Comes the Cud."

Thelma watches, horrified, as Danny opens with a belch before belting out the lyrics. Danny burps. Well, they weren't so much *lyrics* as they were just a list of foods that Danny wants to regurgitate. Each hook ended with a loud *BURP!*

Thelma cringed as she began her verse. It wasn't any better than Danny's verse, but it felt worse to Thelma because her verse wasn't even about her. It was all about Danny and how great he was.

For the grand finale, Danny took back the spotlight and gave one last thunderous *BURP!*

Days later, in Peggy's living room, Peggy, Otis, and Reggie watched the music video in shock, speechless.

Chapter 23

"I never thought I'd have a song at the top of the charts," Thelma said while signing autographs on a stage on the beach, right after their new single hit number one. "This is incredible!"

"Hey," Danny said, greeting a fan begging for an autograph. "There ya go!"

Grinning, Thelma signed autographs for fans and called out, "Hey, hey, y'all! Do the Unicorn! Do the Unicorn! Hey, hey!" The crowd all put their fingers to their foreheads like horns, then spun around to dance like Thelma.

"Thelma! Thelma!" a familiar voice called out from the back of the autograph line.

Thelma looked up. "Reggie?" She was so happy to see her old pal!

"Wow," Reggie said, taking in the crowd surrounding her. "You're like a massive star now! Will you sign this for me?" He passed her a record to sign.

"Are you kidding?" Thelma said, laughing. "Of course, I will!"

Otis suddenly appeared right behind Reggie. Thelma couldn't believe it—the whole band, back together again. "Otis?" she said, grinning. "Oh my goodness! This is amazing! What the heck are you guys doing here?"

"Oh, you know." Otis shrugged. "Peggy booked us a gig down the street."

"Congrats on the new single," Reggie told Thelma. "Danny must be *amazing* to work with." He paused, watching Danny interact with his fans. "Guess what? We just found a new singer!"

"Reggie," Otis said, shushing him. "Be quiet!"

"You did?" Thelma asked, trying not to feel hurt.

"No—" Otis began. "I mean, yes, we did, but—"

Just then, a goat girl ran toward them. "Thelma!" the girl shrieked.

"That's her," Reggie said, pointing at the girl.

"Oh my gosh, oh my gosh," the goat girl said, talking a mile a minute. "Ahhhh! I'm so excited to meet you! I am such a huge fan!" Thelma glanced at Otis, trying to figure out what he was thinking. "Like, I totally wanna cut off one of my horns so I can be just like you."

"Don't you love her?" Reggie asked.

"It's *so* inspiring to meet you," the goat girl yammered on. "Someone that sings her truth! You're, like, the most genuine artist ever."

Thelma and Otis exchanged a look. They both knew there was nothing genuine about this version of Thelma.

A fan called out from the back of the line, "Hey, you're holding up the line!"

Otis stepped away from the table. "Guess we better go," he said quietly. "Take care of yourself, Thelma."

"Well, thanks for stopping by," Thelma said sadly, watching her friends wander off without her. She wanted nothing more than to get up and go with them. They were the truest friends she'd ever had, and they were filled with true talent.

Just as she was considering if she should stand up to follow them, Vic hopped up onstage to make an announcement. “Oh, baby!” he said, calling for the crowd’s attention. “‘Here Comes the Cud’ has just been nominated for Best Music Video of the Year!”

Though the crowd went wild, Thelma had to force herself to smile. It just didn’t feel good to be doing all this without her friends.

Chapter 24

Megan was a woman on a mission. She'd been following Thelma around for days. She was determined to figure out what Thelma was hiding so she could take that unicorn down and put Nikki Narwhal back on top of the charts!

Earlier that day, she'd found a group of unicorn haters, and now it was time to put her plan into action. "Listen up, you weirdos," she said to the group she'd gathered together. "You're the best team I could find for twenty bucks, split six ways. But ain't none of y'all gettin' paid until you push that unicorn to her breaking point—now, go!"

She had to take this unicorn *down*—her boss was depending on it!

As Thelma, Danny, and Vic headed out to the beach boardwalk to celebrate the news that "Here Comes the Cud" had been nominated for Best Music Video of the Year, Megan's unicorn-hating crew was ready to take the trio's celebration down a notch.

From a distance, Megan watched through a telephoto lens, snapping pictures as Thelma, Danny, and Vic roller-skated down the boardwalk. The camera lens was powerful enough that she could zoom in and snap Thelma's expression at the exact moment the first of many eggs pelted her shiny pink coat.

Megan grinned—there was nothing like a good egging to take a girl down. *Go, unicorn haters!* It felt good to see Thelma knocked down a notch.

She continued to snap pictures, gleefully clicking away as eggs continued to zoom at Thelma. One went soaring through the air and flew directly at Thelma's noble unicorn horn. *Splat!* Suddenly, Megan stopped shooting and studied the picture she'd taken at the exact moment of impact. *Hold on a second,* she thought. *Is that horn . . . coming unattached?*

Megan glared at Thelma as she continued to get pelted by eggs. *Just how many secrets is this "unicorn" really hiding?*

Chapter 25

That evening, Thelma was exhausted. It had been a wild day, filled with big news, adoring fans, a surprise visit from her best friends, and *lots* of eggs. She slumped down in her hotel bed and gazed up at the ceiling, trying not to cry. Gosh, she missed those guys.

She rolled onto her side and noticed her songbook sitting on the bedside table. She opened it up, grinning at the picture of the Rusty Buckets she kept inside the book. She sure wished she was with them now, performing as a group again.

She grabbed her phone, debating if she should just call Otis. Why not tell him how much she missed them? But before she was able to dial, her phone buzzed. It was Vic.

"Thelma!" he blurted from the other end of the line. "I've got some amazing news! I've just booked you to headline Sparkle-Palooza in three weeks!"

"What?" Thelma asked, baffled. How was this all happening so fast?

"I told you I'd make it happen!" Vic said. She could practically hear his smile through the phone. "Now get yourself cleaned up. We've got the Music Video Awards tonight!"

A smile crept across her face as she hung up and got ready for the show. She still missed her friends, but this *was* pretty exciting.

Later that night, the Music Video Awards were totally rocking. "The world's hottest musicians have gathered tonight in Hollywood," a news reporter said from the edge of the red carpet, "hoping to win Best Music Video of the Year!"

Nikki Narwhal arrived on the scene, wearing a wig and transported in a special convertible aquarium-limo. She splashed out of the limo, onto the carpet, waving to her fans. No one seemed all that excited to see her. The newscaster went on, "Returning for the first time since her big meltdown is 'Blubber Trouble' superstar, Nikki Narwhal!"

Nikki's Pool Boys danced down the red carpet in front of her, scrubbing the floor so she could more easily slip and slide down the walkway. "I'm baaaaack!" Nikki cheered.

The response was mild. In fact, some people *booed.*

"Alright, you ugly bunch," Nikki shouted. "Look who it is, it's me, *Nikki*!" Megan stood behind her boss, shoving her along the red carpet with a curling broom. "Push, Megan, push!" she ordered.

"I got you, girl!" Megan said, grunting as she shoved Nikki down the red carpet.

When Thelma and Danny's limo pulled up to the start of the red carpet, Danny turned to Thelma and said, "Could you ever imagine our lives would turn out like *this*?"

"Not in a million years," Thelma said.

Danny popped a cowboy hat on top of his head and switched back to his celebrity voice. It was show-time! "Welp! There's no turning back now!"

The crowd went wild when Thelma and Danny stepped out of the limo wearing matching denim outfits. "Hey, get my good side," Danny said, mooning for a camera.

The newscaster announced, "Thelma the Unicorn sent fans into a frenzy today when it was announced that she'll be performing at Sparkle-Palooza."

"I just can't wait to get on that stage," Thelma said, striking her classic unicorn pose.

Nearby, Otis was watching Thelma make her red-carpet debut. "Thelma!" he called out, trying to catch her attention. He wanted her to know that they were there to support her, no matter what. "Over here!"

Thelma couldn't see him through the crowd, but she heard him. "Otis?" she asked, scanning the crowd.

A paparazzo called out to Danny, "Hey! Hey! Who are you wearing?"

Vic answered for them. "We're wearing Fabbio Dongzini."

Just then, Otis managed to poke his head through the crowd. "Thelma!" he called again.

But there was just too much going on, and Thelma never saw him. As photographers swarmed, Vic ushered his two new diamonds inside the theater. "Come on, you little babies," he said.

"Hey," Danny called out to their fans, with one final wave. "Wish us luck! Bye."

Thelma took one last desperate look over her shoulder as they were tucked inside the theater. She'd been *sure* she'd heard Otis, but maybe she was just hearing what she *wished* she could hear.

Chapter 26

Thelma sat in the audience between Vic and Danny, listening to the awards being presented onstage.

"And the award for Best Eyebrows in a Music Video goes to . . . The Trey-Ball Twins!"

Vic nudged Thelma. "Those guys are great." He glanced over at her and gasped—there was a smudge marring her pink complexion. "Oh no!" he whispered loudly. "Thelma, your face is falling apart."

"What?" Thelma asked, horrified.

"I'd run to the bathroom and fix it," Vic suggested. "Our category's almost up!"

Thelma pulled out her makeup mirror and glanced at herself. Vic was right. The pink paint around her lips had been rubbed off, exposing her real color! She raced out of the auditorium in a panic.

In the bathroom, she pulled her pink touch-up paint out of her purse and got to work. Just as she finished, Megan burst out of one of the stalls. "Hello, Thelma," Nikki's assistant said, causing Thelma to jump in alarm. She hadn't realized anyone else was in the bathroom.

"Ooh, girl!" Thelma said, calming herself. "You scared the jelly beans outta me. You just been . . . hanging out in there?" She nodded toward the stall.

Megan strutted toward Thelma, passing her a large envelope. "Here," she said. "I just wanted to give you this."

"Oh," Thelma said, glancing at the envelope in her hooves. "Uh, okay, thanks." She opened the envelope. Inside were dozens of photos of her unicorn horn coming unattached during the egging on the boardwalk.

"It's funny," Megan said. "I didn't know unicorn horns could detach themselves like that."

"What?" Thelma gasped. "Why are you doing this?"

Megan laughed. "Because I'll do anything to get

Nikki back on top!" Suddenly, Megan doused Thelma with a bucket full of paint thinner.

All traces of pink paint melted away, and the impact of the splash knocked off Thelma's horn. She stood, helpless, in a puddle of pink sludge. Megan laughed while filming video of Thelma returning to her natural state.

Megan bent down to collect Thelma's horn off the ground. "A carrot?" she asked, holding the carrot in midair as glitter drizzled off it. "Your magic horn was a carrot? Ha! I knew there was no such thing as unicorns."

"Please," Thelma begged. "I—I can explain."

"Oh, that won't be necessary," Megan said, shoving her phone in front of Thelma's face to show her the video she'd captured. "After I post this video, the whole world will know what you really are: just a phony little pony." She laughed again, feeling both proud and relieved—she'd done it! She'd uncovered Thelma's secrets and was going to take her down! "Oh man, I can't wait to see the look on everyone's stupid faces when they find out how you've betrayed them."

"Megan, please don't do this," Thelma begged. "I

can't go back to the way things were. I'll give you anything you want."

"Too late for that, Thelma," Megan tsked. She held up her phone victoriously. "Time for the world to see you as the pathetic creature you are." She hovered her finger over the post button.

"Wait! Stop!" Thelma screamed. "Don't!" She sighed, knowing there was only one thing that might get Megan to cancel her post. "Just—just let me disappear. You'll never see or hear from me ever again. It'll be like I never existed."

Megan considered the offer. "Fine. But I want you gone for *good.* Because if you ever try to come back, you know exactly what will happen to you." She wiggled her phone in the air again. "Bye-bye, now."

Thelma was close to tears but wanted to hold it together until she was alone. With a sad sigh, she tossed her outfit in the garbage, glanced at herself in the mirror, and headed for the exit.

Chapter 27

Now that she was back to being a plain farm pony, Thelma was able to trot down the awards show hallway without being recognized. She could hear Vic calling for her, but she had to go—Megan had given her no choice. "Thelma! Thelma?" she could hear Vic yelling as she hustled toward the exit. "Where are you? Excuse me, have you seen a tiny pink unicorn? Loves to sing about farts and acid reflux?" Thelma carried on, though Vic's voice continued to ring out behind her as he asked people if they'd seen her. "Thelma, please, come to Vicky! Thelma!"

Just as Thelma reached the door that led out to the street, she heard someone onstage announcing, "And the winner for Best Music Video of the Year goes to . . ." She cocked her head, curious to hear the result. ". . . 'Here Comes the Cud' by Danny Stallion and Thelma the Unicorn!" With a sad sigh, Thelma pushed the door open and slipped outside into the big wide world where she would be a nobody once again.

Inside the theater, Danny was confused. "Uh . . . where'd she go?"

Nearby, Megan slid into her seat and whispered to Nikki, "Mission accomplished." She tossed the carrot horn to Nikki, who rewarded her with a high five.

"Nice one," Nikki told her.

"You'll be back on top in a week," Megan said proudly.

Suddenly, Vic screamed out from the back of the auditorium, "Blasted! Thelma's missing!" The whole crowd gasped. "I don't mean to alarm you, but we seem to have lost Thelma. Now, will everyone please take a moment and look under your seats for her? She's a unicorn, she's quite small—she may have gotten trapped under your butt . . ."

Danny looked under his seat. No Thelma.

Meanwhile, word had reached the fans outside the awards show that Thelma was missing. Otis quickly set out to try to find his friend. Though he didn't see her, he did find *something* during his hunt—Thelma's songbook! He pulled it out of a trash can near a bus stop that was just outside the theater. He pulled it out just as a bus wheezed into motion and drove away from the stop. Otis couldn't guess where Thelma was going, but he knew there was something truly wrong if she'd left her songbook in the trash . . .

Chapter 28

The hunt for Thelma the Unicorn was on.

"The entire world is in mourning after learning about the sudden disappearance of Thelma the Unicorn," a news reporter announced over the TV after Thelma had been missing for several days.

As the TV flashed through scenes of grieving fans gathering for candlelight vigils and the coverage of extensive missing-unicorn hunts, the reporter went on. "Volunteers everywhere are desperately trying to find Thelma in any way they can. It suddenly feels like all magic and hope have been lost in the world."

Things didn't improve over the next few weeks. As

far as the music world was concerned, Thelma the Unicorn was well and truly gone.

Thelma had done a great job of hiding. She'd headed as far from Hollywood as her four feet would carry her and was trotting aimlessly through the desert, trying to figure out her next move. What's a pony supposed to do after going from no one, to someone, then back to no one in just a matter of weeks?

As she considered this, a trucker pulled up alongside her and rolled down his window. Thelma looked up to see who had stopped her. It was the trucker, driving the paint-and-glitter truck that had started this whole thing in the first place! "Hey, horse lady," the trucker called. "Ya need a ride?"

Recovering from her shock, Thelma hopped up into the truck. Thelma wouldn't normally accept rides from strangers, but this was an emergency.

"So, uh, where ya headed, kid?" the trucker asked her as he rambled down the road.

"Maybe the next rest stop." Thelma sighed. "So I can flush myself down the toilet."

"Welp." The trucker laughed. "I've heard that one before!" He glanced over at Thelma, then swerved to keep his truck from veering off the road. "You know, being on the road makes you wanna ponder, and I ponder a lot. I might as well call my brain the *ponderosa.* Hey, you mind if I ask you a question?" He slurped a sip of his soda, once again nearly careening off the road.

"Uh, no," Thelma said with a shrug. "Go ahead."

"You ever wake up and realize you've been livin' a lie?"

Thelma stared at him. "Boy, do I know what that's like."

"Here's the deal," the trucker said, knocking over a few garbage cans on the side of the road as he settled his soda back into the cup holder. "I just got engaged to the woman of my dreams. But I've been keepin' a huge secret from her."

"Really?" Thelma asked. "What is it?"

The trucker began to pay even less attention to the road ahead, which troubled Thelma. But the guy clearly had some stuff to unload, and she figured hearing his troubles would help her forget about some of her own. "Well," he began, swerving just enough to narrowly miss a row of construction cones. "I'm a world-famous champion on the underground clogging circuit." He dug under his seat, unearthing a laptop. With one hand barely on the wheel, he opened the laptop and showed Thelma a clogging video.

"There's an underground clogging circuit?" Thelma asked.

"We have dance battles in sewers and old grain silos," the trucker explained. "My fans call me Gregory Thunder Calves. Given the fact that my calves are so big."

Thelma stared at him, baffled. "So, what's the big deal? Like, why don't you just tell your fiancée the truth?"

"Well," the trucker said, shrugging, "I'm just afraid, I guess. I mean, what if she hates clogging and totally rejects me?"

Thelma shook her head. "Look, if she really loves you, then she should love everything about you . . . even the clogging."

The trucker's face lit up at this suggestion. "You really think so?"

Thelma thought for a moment. "I mean, I hope so. No matter what happens, it's gonna be better than spending the rest of your life living a lie. You're perfect just as you are."

"Wow!" the trucker said, impressed at Thelma's

confidence. "You must have, like, zero problems in your life."

Thelma suddenly realized that *she* needed her own advice more than anyone. "Stop the truck!" she screamed.

The trucker slammed on the brakes. "Something's up, ain't it?" he asked.

"We need to turn around," Thelma told him, frantic. "I need to go back to the farm!"

"Well," the trucker said, whipping his truck in a sharp U-turn. "Let me just put the old turn signal on!"

Chapter 29

Otis was busy hanging up missing posters outside his and Thelma's favorite café when he suddenly spotted the paint-and-glitter truck—the very same one that had started this whole mess with Thelma and Vic and the broken Rusty Buckets in the first place—zooming away. When the dust settled, Otis saw the most amazing surprise heading toward him. "Thelma?" It was his best friend! "Thelma!" He dropped his posters and rushed over to hug her. "Where have you been? I've been searching all over for you! Are—are you okay?"

"I'm fine, Otis," Thelma assured him. "I'm fine."

"I've just been so worried about you," Otis told her.

"I know you have. But I don't deserve it." Thelma

smiled at her best bud. "I should never have left you guys."

"It's okay," Otis said, and he meant it. "You're back now!"

Thelma shook her head sadly. "No, it's not okay. I screwed up big-time. I thought being a unicorn would make all my dreams come true . . . but instead, I lost the people who loved me the most."

"Stop it, Thelma," Otis said, trying to hide his grin. "You're making me blush."

"No, seriously," she said, swatting him. "I'd be happy playing music anywhere. As long as it's with *you*."

"Thanks, Thelma," Otis said.

"You were right all along . . ." Thelma said. "I've gotta come clean now."

Otis looked at her, wide-eyed. "Wait, are you serious?"

"It's time to show everyone who the real Thelma is," she said.

Otis howled with excitement. Then he pulled a carrot from the vegetable stand outside the café. "Are you sure you don't wanna wear this bad boy again?" He switched into a silly voice and pretended the carrot was talking. *"Put me on your head, Thelma!"*

"Get that nasty thing outta my face," Thelma said, swatting the carrot away.

Just then, Gerald pulled up alongside them in his old El Camino with Reggie in the back of the truck. "Thelma!" Reggie whooped. "We've been looking everywhere for you!"

"What's up, Reggie?" she asked.

Peggy Purvis leaned out of the truck's front passenger window. "Hi, Thelma!"

"Peggy!" Thelma said, running over to give her a hug. "I'm so sorry. I never shoulda left you—"

"Don't worry about it, kid," Peggy said with a wave. "I knew you'd come around."

"I'm sure you've already heard, but I'm not really a unicorn," she told Peggy.

"Girl," Peggy said, shrugging. "I smelled paint on you from the very beginning."

Thelma laughed. "Come on, everyone. Sparkle-Palooza is about to begin, and no one's stopping us from getting on that stage."

Everyone cheered. Thelma and Otis climbed into the back with Reggie. Just as they settled into their spots, Otis passed something to Thelma. It was her songbook! "Hey," he said, nudging it into her hooves. "I think you're gonna need this."

Chapter 30

"Thousands of fans from all over the globe have gathered for Sparkle-Palooza, the biggest music event of the year!" a reporter outside the stadium announced, signaling for her camera guy to catch shots of the endless sea of unicorn fans, all of whom were wearing horns like Thelma's. "And while the world still mourns the disappearance of Thelma the Unicorn, music's top stars have shown up to perform in her stead."

Onstage, Danny Stallion was lip-synching with his new boy band, while Vic Diamond grooved along from inside the sound booth.

"But many of Thelma's fans," the reporter went on,

"are still holding out hope that their beloved pink unicorn will return . . ."

Overhead, a helicopter zoomed through the sky, carrying Nikki Narwhal in a giant sparkly sling. "What up, land dwellers!" Nikki boomed. "Are you ready for this?"

The reporter carried on with her report. "In the meantime, Nikki Narwhal is back! Here to reclaim her crown as the original Queen of Pop!"

Music blared out of the speakers along the edges of the stage as Nikki was lowered from the sky. "Thank you!" she called out to the crowd spread out ahead of her. "Thank you so much! Thank you!"

While Nikki took her spot onstage, Megan was making sure things were all squared away backstage. She lectured a few of her unicorn-hating crew and an ostrich security guard about the plan. "Listen, if any of you morons see anyone pretending to be Thelma, I want you to notify me immediately. Any questions?"

The security ostrich raised his wing. "Is now a bad time to order a stuffed-crust pizza?"

"I told y'all to eat before you came," Megan barked. "Now get out there and do your jobs!"

"I love my job!" the ostrich clucked.

Just as Megan's group fanned out to keep watch for Thelma, Megan. Gerald pulled his El Camino up to the security gate outside the stadium. A security bear was busy playing a video game and didn't seem to notice the group at the gate.

"Reggie," Otis whispered from inside the truck as Reggie popped out. "Are you sure this is gonna work?"

"Just trust me," Reggie said. He crept up to a fence with a lock on it.

Gerald pulled his car forward, so he was idling right behind Reggie at the fence. "How are we going to get in?" Gerald asked, sizing up the lock on the gate.

"Don't worry." Reggie grinned. "I know how to pick locks." He smashed the lock with a hammer, then announced, "Let's roll!"

As soon as they were safely inside the fence, Thelma and Otis spilled out.

"You guys better hurry," Gerald told them. "You've got bogeys at your twelve o'clock."

Thelma spotted a security guard at the exact same moment he noticed her. "Hey! What do you think you're doing here?" the guard yelled at them. He pulled out a walkie-talkie and announced, "Intruders! I repeat, intruders! Requesting backup!"

As the security guard brigade rushed past her, Peggy stuck her cane out and whooped them, in order to give Thelma and Otis a head start.

"Attagirl, Peg!" Gerald cheered.

Thelma and Otis stared, shocked at what Peggy had just done. She ushered them on, yelling out, "What y'all doin'? Get goin'! We'll hold 'em off!"

"Follow me," Thelma said, grabbing Otis and dragging him after her. Reggie was close on their heels. "We gotta get to the stage!"

Megan was scanning the security monitors just as the message came through on her walkie-talkie. "Be on the lookout for a pony and a couple of donkey boys!"

"What?" Megan screeched. She leaned in closer to the monitor for a better look. It was them! But how on earth did they get in?

She took out her phone to post the video, but the phone battery blinked at her, dying as she looked at it. Her eyes narrowing, she grabbed a taser gun from one of the security guards and hightailed it out of the surveillance room. It was time to take matters into her own hands.

Chapter 31

"It's straight ahead!" Thelma said, leading Otis and Reggie through a tunnel under the stage.

"Freeze!" called out a security guard, stepping right into Thelma's path. "Don't move!"

Thelma and her friends took a sharp turn, heading in a different direction. As they ran, Thelma called back over her shoulder, "Come on, *Donk-Truvius* . . . Show us what you got!"

Otis grinned and slipped into his special role-playing voice. "The pleasure is all mine." Then he grabbed a guitar, leapt into the air, and struck a ceiling water pipe. "Ha!" he called, cheering as water sprayed onto the floor. But his cheer turned into a muffled scream as the guards who were chasing them slipped on the water, and instead of falling behind, they crashed into the band—pushing Thelma, Otis, and Reggie straight into a storage room.

The door slammed behind them, and Thelma heard it lock.

"Hey! Open up in there!" a security guard called from the other side.

"What do we do now?" Otis asked quietly.

"Nothing," said a voice from across the small storage room. "You're trapped."

Through the dim, Thelma spotted Megan and Nikki Narwhal hidden in the shadows. Megan was holding out a taser, while Nikki wormed her way toward them. "You really thought you could just prance right in here and steal my thunder again?" Nikki growled.

"No," Thelma said. "Nikki, I swear!"

"Well, news flash, Thelma," Nikki said. "You're nothing without your sparkles. You're just a worthless little pony that no one wants to listen to. I'm the *real* horned superstar!"

Thelma had to admit that it stung to hear someone say that out loud.

“Boom!” Megan snapped. “Nikki’s the real tuna, not some canned substitute!”

“Nikki, please,” Thelma begged. “We don’t want no trouble—”

Nikki cut her off. “You really want to sparkle again?”

“This should do the trick,” Megan said, thrusting the taser forward. But just before she could fire it, Thelma kicked a mop bucket toward them. The mop hit Megan in the head, throwing her off her aim. The taser prongs zoomed past Thelma and struck an electrical box instead, activating some kind of hydraulic platform.

As Thelma and her band were lifted up toward the ceiling of the storage room, sparks zipped and popped in the air around their heads. Megan jumped for the platform and grabbed hold of Otis’s hoof. She tried to pull him off, but Thelma was stronger and was able to keep him up on the still-lifting platform. “Oh, no you don’t! Girl, you ain’t breakin’ up this band!”

She tugged Otis one more time and Megan lost hold of Otis’s foot. She fell back, off the platform, landing right on Nikki’s blowhole—butt-first, where she got stuck. “Oof!” Nikki grunted.

Meanwhile, Thelma and the Rusty Buckets

continued to rise up into the ceiling. It opened above them, revealing the backstage area of the Sparkle-Palooza stage!

Otis nudged Thelma and said, "We're finally here, Thelma! Sparkle-Palooza . . ."

The platform had delivered them up to a special area just behind the Sparkle-Palooza main stage. Thelma could hear the crowd chanting through the curtain in front of them. "Hey," she said to her two friends. "Uh, I'll be right back. There's something I gotta do."

As Thelma darted away, Otis called after her, "Hey, wait, wait, wait, Thelma—"

Just then, the curtain in front of Otis and Reggie swung open. Otis blinked against the blaring lights and massive crowd spread out before them. The chanting stopped and the audience stared at the two donkeys who were now standing center stage in the stadium.

"Who are those guys?" a lady yelled from the audience.

Someone else called, "Boo! Get off the stage!"

"What should we do?" Reggie asked helplessly.

"I don't know," Otis replied.

Just as a hush went over the entire stadium, a small voice—Suzie, the girl who'd first found Thelma the day she was showered in glitter—rang out from somewhere in the stadium: "Thelma?"

Otis and Reggie both turned, and their mouths dropped open. There was Thelma, dressed once again as a pink unicorn. The crowd went still, then a huge cheer went up when all the fans realized what this meant: Thelma the Unicorn was back!

Thelma walked toward the microphone, passing her two friends.

"What are you doing?" Otis whispered.

Slowly, Thelma stepped up to the microphone. "Hey, everybody," she said. "I know you must be wondering where I've been all this time. I don't blame you. I've been wondering that myself. Ever since I was little, I always dreamed about performing on this stage." She glanced around the Sparkle-Palooza stage, taking it all in—the crowd, the lights, the magic.

Thelma went on, "But I never thought I'd make it here because of how I looked. Something inside me kept telling me I wasn't good enough." She took a deep breath. "Then one day, this crazy thing happened, and everyone finally started paying attention to me." After a pause, Thelma said, "But it's not who I really am."

Reaching up to the top of her head, Thelma snapped off her sparkly unicorn horn. Then she took out a rag and started wiping the pink paint off her body. The crowd gasped as Thelma was transformed—from a magical unicorn into a plain farm pony.

"This is the real me," Thelma said into the mic. "I'm Thelma." She locked eyes with Suzie and said, "I'm really sorry. I never meant to hurt anyone; I just thought it was the only way people would give my music a chance."

The crowd listened, stunned, as Thelma shared her truth. "And now I'd like to share a song with you. I started writing it when I was a kid. I just never knew what I needed to say until now."

Otis grinned at his pal. Thelma smiled back at both him and Reggie and said, "Alright, guys, let's do this."

Thelma smiled again and looked out at the crowd. "Dare not look behind you; you've come too far. Let the tears you've shed remind you of who you really are. You've searched the entire world just to find everything you needed was right inside."

Otis and the rest of the band joined in as Thelma continued singing, her voice becoming bold and confident. As the song progressed, the crowd began cheering, waving their unicorn lights in the air. Even the Pool Boys couldn't help but bust out their best moves.

"So turn your light on," Thelma sang out to the sea of unicorn-shaped stars. "Let us see who you are, one in a million. No one's playing your part. Don't be perfect. Like the moon and the stars, you shine just as you are."

Inside the storage room, Nikki and Megan watched Thelma and the Rusty Buckets' song on Nikki's phone. Nikki swiped away a tear, realizing how wrong she'd been about Thelma—this pony's talent was legit! In a show of solidarity, Nikki ripped off her own horn. She had also been pretending to be someone she wasn't all along, just like Thelma!

"Nikki, darling," Vic said, approaching Nikki Narwhal and Megan. "I've just become available to manage you again—"

Nikki rolled her eyes and turned away, blowing water at Vic through her blowhole.

Back onstage, Otis wandered over to Thelma. Together, they gazed out across the sea of fans as fireworks exploded overhead. Otis put his arm around

Thelma as Reggie cheered. "Hey, Otis," Reggie called out. "Do you know what time it is?"

"Ooh, I know what time it is," Otis said. "Thelma, do *you* know what time it is?"

Thelma backed up, ran, and leapt off the stage. She soared over the crowd, knowing that—this time—the open arms of the fans below would be there to catch her.

Chapter 32

Not long after their Sparkle-Palooza debut, things were finally going back to normal—the new normal, that is: the one where the Rusty Buckets were famous even though Thelma was rocking her brown fur once again. She and Otis sat together under a tree, playing a game of Dungeons & Wagons during a recording break.

"Ouch," Otis said, cringing after Thelma rolled a pair of twenty-sided dice.

"Whaddya mean, *ouch*?" Thelma asked, shooting him a look. "I just rolled a thirty-two!"

"Well," Otis explained. "A half orc with super low intelligence just stole eighty pounds of your corn bread."

Thelma squinted. "Well, can't I just poop out some jelly beans?"

"Technically, yes," Otis said. "But you also have dysentery. So, they might be *dubious beans*."

Peggy Purvis called out to them from across the field. She was standing in front of the group's new recording studio, which they'd officially named Sparkle Studios. "Break time's over," Peggy yelled. "We've got an album to finish!"

"Be right there, Peggy," Thelma yelled back.

Otis and Thelma began to trot across the field to return to the studio when a voice called out from the other side of the fence. It was Zirconia, one of the prancing ponies from next door. "Thelma!" she called out. "Can we take a picture with you?"

"Of course," Thelma said, heading toward Zirconia and her crew.

"Okay, everyone," Otis said, framing up the shot with his cell phone. "Let's squeeze in just a little closer."

Zirconia wiggled with excitement. "Oh, I cannot believe that this is happening! Girl, I ain't got no more pink eye!"

"Okay," Otis said, lining the phone up. "Perfect. Big smiles on three . . ."

Just then, a huge truck hauling glue and swan feathers came barreling down the road.

"Two . . ." Otis said, not noticing that they were right in the path of a very out-of-control truck. Just before Otis could say *one*, the trucker hit a pothole, his straw lodged itself into his nose, and the truck veered and lurched.

". . . and one!" Otis said, just as Thelma noticed the truck heading their way. She gasped.

The truck leapt into the air and the back popped open. In the next second, glue and feathers flew everywhere, filling the air around them.

When things had settled, Thelma glanced over at her best friend—and then began to laugh. Because Otis had been coated in glue and feathers and now looked exactly like a stunning Pegasus.

"What?" Otis asked, while Thelma continued to laugh. First, Thelma had turned into a unicorn, now Otis was a Pegasus?

Maybe it was time to start their *next* adventure!